Gluten free
Cookbook
For college students

Easy and delicious recipes on a budget

Judy Kelly

Gluten free Cookbook
For college students

Easy and delicious recipes on a budget

Judy Kelly

All rights reserved. No part of this publication may be reproduced, distributed, or transmitted in any form or by any means, including photocopying, recording, or other electronic or mechanical methods, without the prior written permission of the publisher, except in the case of brief quotations embodied in critical reviews and certain other noncommercial uses permitted by copyright law.

Copyright © Judy Kelly, 2023.

Table of Contents

Introduction..5

Chapter 1: Understanding Gluten-Free Eating..8

Chapter 2: Kitchen Essentials for Gluten-Free Cooking.................................. 23

Chapter 3: Breakfast and Brunch Recipes. 37

Chapter 4: Lunch and Dinner Recipes........49

Chapter 5: Snacks and Sides...................... 66

Chapter 6: Desserts and Treats................... 79

Chapter 7: Meal Planning And Tips............ 91

Conclusion... 97

Introduction

Welcome to "The Gluten-Free Cookbook for College Students: Easy and Delicious Recipes on a Budget"! College life can be exciting and challenging, and for those who follow a gluten-free diet, finding affordable and tasty meal options can sometimes feel like an additional hurdle. But fear not, because this cookbook is designed specifically for you.

Whether you're a freshman navigating your way through the college dining halls or a busy senior juggling classes, assignments, and a limited budget, this cookbook is here to help you make delicious gluten-free meals without breaking the bank. We understand the importance of eating well to fuel your body and mind, and we believe that being gluten-free shouldn't limit your ability to enjoy flavorful and satisfying dishes.

In this cookbook, we will not only provide you with a variety of easy-to-follow recipes but also equip you with the knowledge and tips necessary to understand gluten-free eating and navigate the challenges of college life. We want to empower you to take charge of your own dietary needs, even with a busy student schedule and limited resources.

Whether you are new to gluten-free cooking or have been following this lifestyle for a while, this cookbook aims to inspire you with creative and affordable recipes that will tantalize your taste buds. From breakfast and brunch options to hearty lunches, dinners, snacks, and even desserts, we have you covered with a diverse range of dishes that are both wholesome and flavorful.

Additionally, we will guide you on setting up a gluten-free pantry, understanding food labels, and making smart choices while grocery shopping. We know that being a college student often means working with a tight budget, so we will share tips and tricks to help you make the most of your money without compromising on taste or nutrition.

So, get ready to embark on a culinary adventure that celebrates delicious gluten-free cooking while keeping your budget intact. Whether you're cooking for yourself or hosting a gathering with friends, "The Gluten-Free Cookbook for College Students" is your go-to resource for satisfying meals that won't break the bank. Let's dive in and discover how gluten-free eating can be easy, enjoyable, and affordable for every college student.

Chapter 1: Understanding Gluten-Free Eating

1.1 What is Gluten?

Gluten is a term that you might have come across if you follow a gluten-free diet or have encountered gluten-free products in grocery stores or restaurants. But what exactly is gluten?

In simple terms, gluten is a mixture of proteins found in certain grains, particularly wheat, barley, and rye. It acts as a binding agent, giving dough its elasticity and providing structure to baked goods. Gluten gives bread its chewy texture and helps it rise during baking, creating a fluffy and airy result.

Gluten is made up of two main proteins: gliadin and glutenin. When these proteins come into contact with water, they form a sticky, elastic network that gives bread and other wheat-based products their characteristic texture. This unique property of gluten makes it highly desirable in baking and food production.

However, for some individuals, consuming gluten can have adverse effects on their health. People with celiac disease, an autoimmune disorder, have a severe intolerance to gluten. When individuals with celiac disease consume gluten, their immune system reacts by damaging the lining of the small intestine, leading to various gastrointestinal symptoms and malabsorption of nutrients.

Apart from celiac disease, some people may also have non-celiac gluten sensitivity. This condition is characterized by similar symptoms to celiac disease, such as bloating, abdominal pain, and fatigue, but without the same immune system response or intestinal damage. For these individuals, eliminating gluten from their diet can alleviate their symptoms and improve their overall well-being.

It's important to note that gluten is not inherently harmful or unhealthy for most people. In fact, whole grains containing gluten, such as wheat, can be a part of a balanced diet and provide essential nutrients like fiber, vitamins, and minerals. However, for those with celiac disease or non-celiac gluten sensitivity, avoiding gluten is crucial to maintaining their health and well-being.

With the increasing awareness of gluten-related disorders and the rise in gluten-free diets, there are now a wide variety of gluten-free alternatives available in the market. These alternatives use grains like rice, corn, quinoa, and gluten-free oats, along with various gluten-free flours and starches, to mimic the properties of gluten in baking and cooking.

Understanding what gluten is and its effects on different individuals is essential for making informed choices about your dietary needs. Whether you follow a gluten-free diet out of necessity or personal preference, being knowledgeable about gluten and its sources will help you navigate food options and create delicious meals that cater to your specific needs.

1.2 Gluten-Free Diet Basics

Following a gluten-free diet involves avoiding foods and ingredients that contain gluten. This can be a significant lifestyle change, but with the right knowledge and preparation, it is entirely manageable. Here are some basics to help you understand and navigate a gluten-free diet:

1. Gluten-Free Foods: When following a gluten-free diet, it's important to focus on naturally gluten-free foods. These include fruits, vegetables, lean proteins, dairy products, legumes, nuts, and gluten-free grains like rice, quinoa, corn, and gluten-free oats. These foods are safe to consume and form the foundation of a well-balanced gluten-free diet.

2. Gluten-Containing Foods to Avoid: It's crucial to identify and avoid foods that contain gluten. The primary sources of gluten are wheat, barley, rye, and their derivatives. This means you should steer clear of products such as wheat-based bread, pasta, cereals, pastries, crackers, and baked goods. Additionally, some processed

foods, condiments, sauces, and soups may contain hidden sources of gluten, so it's important to carefully read ingredient labels.

3. Cross-Contamination: Cross-contamination occurs when gluten-free foods come into contact with gluten-containing foods or surfaces. Even trace amounts of gluten can trigger a reaction in individuals with celiac disease or gluten sensitivity. To prevent cross-contamination, it's essential to thoroughly clean utensils, cutting boards, and cooking surfaces before preparing gluten-free meals. Using separate toasters and designated gluten-free cooking tools can also help minimize the risk.

4. Gluten-Free Labeling: Look for products labeled "gluten-free" or those with a gluten-free certification symbol. The "gluten-free" label indicates that the product meets specific standards and contains less than 20 parts per million (ppm) of gluten, which is considered safe for most individuals with gluten-related disorders. However, it's still important to read

the ingredient list to ensure that there are no hidden sources of gluten.

5. Gluten-Free Alternatives: Fortunately, there is a wide range of gluten-free alternatives available for common gluten-containing foods. You can find gluten-free bread, pasta, flour blends, and baking mixes in most grocery stores or specialty health food stores. Experimenting with different gluten-free grains and flours can open up a world of delicious possibilities in your gluten-free cooking and baking.

6. Meal Planning and Preparation: Planning your meals in advance can simplify the process of following a gluten-free diet. Research and gather gluten-free recipes, create shopping lists, and meal prep whenever possible. By having gluten-free options readily available, you'll be less likely to resort to convenience foods that may contain hidden gluten.

7. Seek Support and Guidance: It can be helpful to connect with support groups or online

communities where you can share experiences, get advice, and find support from others following a gluten-free lifestyle. Consulting with a registered dietitian who specializes in gluten-free diets can also provide personalized guidance and help ensure you're meeting your nutritional needs.

Remember, maintaining a gluten-free diet requires diligence, label reading, and awareness of potential sources of gluten. With time, it will become easier to identify safe food choices and adapt your cooking and dining habits. Embracing a gluten-free lifestyle can lead to improved health, increased energy levels, and a renewed enjoyment of food.

1.3 Benefits of a Gluten-Free Lifestyle
Adopting a gluten-free lifestyle has gained significant popularity in recent years, with many people choosing to follow this dietary approach for various reasons. While a gluten-free lifestyle is essential for individuals with celiac disease or non-celiac gluten sensitivity, there are also

potential benefits that extend beyond these specific medical conditions. Here are some potential benefits of a gluten-free lifestyle:

1. Relief from Digestive Issues: For individuals with celiac disease or gluten sensitivity, eliminating gluten from their diet can lead to significant relief from digestive symptoms such as bloating, abdominal pain, diarrhea, and constipation. Removing gluten allows the small intestine to heal in individuals with celiac disease and reduces inflammation in those with gluten sensitivity.

2. Improved Nutrient Absorption: Celiac disease can impair the absorption of essential nutrients from food, leading to deficiencies in vitamins, minerals, and other vital nutrients. By following a gluten-free diet, individuals with celiac disease can allow their intestines to heal and improve nutrient absorption, leading to better overall health and well-being.

3. Increased Energy Levels: Some individuals report increased energy levels and reduced fatigue after transitioning to a gluten-free diet. This could be due to the elimination of gluten-triggered inflammation or the improved absorption of nutrients necessary for optimal energy production.

4. Enhanced Digestive Health: Gluten-containing foods can be difficult for some individuals to digest, even without celiac disease or gluten sensitivity. By avoiding gluten, they may experience improved digestion and fewer digestive discomforts, leading to better overall digestive health.

5. Weight Management: Following a gluten-free diet may support weight management goals for some individuals. However, it's important to note that not all gluten-free foods are automatically healthier or lower in calories. Choosing whole, unprocessed gluten-free foods like fruits, vegetables, lean proteins, and

gluten-free grains can contribute to a balanced and nutritious diet.

6. Increased Variety in Food Choices: Adopting a gluten-free lifestyle can encourage individuals to explore a wider variety of foods and ingredients. It opens up opportunities to try alternative grains and experiment with new recipes, leading to a more diverse and exciting culinary experience.

7. Mindful Eating and Nutritional Awareness: When following a gluten-free lifestyle, individuals tend to become more mindful of their food choices and read ingredient labels more carefully. This increased awareness can lead to a better understanding of the nutritional content of foods and promote healthier overall eating habits.

It's important to note that while a gluten-free lifestyle can offer these potential benefits, it may not be necessary or beneficial for everyone. For individuals without gluten-related disorders, there is no strong scientific evidence to support widespread adoption of a gluten-free diet. It's always recommended to consult with a healthcare professional or registered dietitian before making significant changes to your diet to ensure it aligns with your specific needs and health goals.

Ultimately, the decision to follow a gluten-free lifestyle should be based on individual circumstances, health conditions, and personal preferences.

1.4 Tips for Eating Gluten-Free on a Budget

Eating gluten-free on a budget doesn't have to be a daunting task. With careful planning, smart shopping, and some creative strategies, you can maintain a gluten-free lifestyle without breaking the bank. Here are some tips to help you eat gluten-free on a budget:

1. Embrace Whole, Unprocessed Foods: Focus on incorporating whole, naturally gluten-free foods into your diet. Fruits, vegetables, lean

proteins, legumes, nuts, and gluten-free grains like rice, quinoa, and corn are typically more affordable than specialty gluten-free products. These foods provide essential nutrients and can form the foundation of a budget-friendly gluten-free diet.

2. Cook from Scratch: Pre-packaged gluten-free products can be expensive. By preparing meals and snacks from scratch, you can save money and have better control over the ingredients. Simple, homemade meals using basic ingredients tend to be more budget-friendly and can be just as delicious and nutritious.

3. Buy in Bulk: Purchasing gluten-free staples in bulk can be a cost-effective strategy. Look for bulk bins or larger packages of gluten-free grains, flours, nuts, and seeds. Buying in bulk not only saves money but also ensures you have a steady supply of gluten-free ingredients.

4. Plan Your Meals and Make a Shopping List: Plan your meals for the week ahead and create a

shopping list based on your meal plan. This helps you avoid impulse purchases and ensures you have all the necessary ingredients on hand. Planning meals also reduces food waste and saves money in the long run.

5. Shop the Perimeter of the Store: The outer aisles of the grocery store typically contain fresh produce, meats, dairy, and other whole foods. These are the sections where you'll find many naturally gluten-free options. Focus your shopping on these areas to minimize the need for expensive gluten-free specialty items.

6. Compare Prices and Shop Sales: Take the time to compare prices and check for sales or discounts on gluten-free products. Consider shopping at multiple stores to find the best deals. Online shopping platforms and newsletters from grocery stores can also provide information on special promotions or discounts.

7. Utilize Coupons and Loyalty Programs: Look for coupons or digital deals for gluten-free

products. Many grocery stores have loyalty programs or email newsletters that offer discounts on specific items. Take advantage of these savings opportunities to reduce your grocery expenses.

8. Meal Prep and Freeze: Batch cooking and meal prepping can save both time and money. Cook large batches of gluten-free meals and freeze individual portions for later use. This helps prevent food waste and provides convenient, cost-effective meals when you're short on time or energy.

9. Make Your Own Gluten-Free Staples: Instead of buying expensive gluten-free bread, pasta, or baked goods, consider making your own. Gluten-free bread mixes, pizza dough, and baking mixes are often more affordable than pre-packaged options. Plus, homemade versions can be customized to suit your taste preferences.

10. Join Support Groups and Online Communities: Connect with others following a

gluten-free diet through support groups or online communities. These platforms often share budget-friendly tips, recipes, and product recommendations. Learning from others' experiences can help you discover cost-saving strategies and affordable gluten-free options.

Remember, eating gluten-free on a budget requires some initial planning and research, but it is entirely possible. By prioritizing whole, unprocessed foods, shopping strategically, and being resourceful in the kitchen, you can maintain a healthy gluten-free diet while keeping your finances in check.

Chapter 2: Kitchen Essentials for Gluten-Free Cooking

2.1 Stocking a Gluten-Free Pantry

Stocking a gluten-free pantry is essential for anyone following a gluten-free lifestyle. Having a well-stocked pantry ensures that you always have gluten-free ingredients on hand to create delicious meals and snacks. Here are some key items to consider when stocking your gluten-free pantry:

1. Gluten-Free Grains: Replace gluten-containing grains like wheat, barley, and rye with gluten-free alternatives. Stock up on gluten-free grains such as rice (both white and brown), quinoa, millet, cornmeal, gluten-free oats, amaranth, and sorghum. These grains serve as versatile staples for a variety of dishes.

2. Gluten-Free Flours and Starches: Gluten-free baking requires alternative flours and starches.

Consider having a selection of gluten-free flours such as rice flour, almond flour, coconut flour, tapioca flour/starch, potato starch, and cornstarch. These can be used in various recipes and provide the necessary structure and texture in gluten-free baking.

3. Gluten-Free Pasta and Noodles: Stock your pantry with gluten-free pasta options made from rice, corn, quinoa, or other gluten-free grains. Having different shapes and varieties of gluten-free pasta allows you to enjoy your favorite pasta dishes without compromising on taste or texture.

4. Condiments and Sauces: Many condiments and sauces contain hidden sources of gluten. Check labels carefully and opt for gluten-free versions of soy sauce, tamari, Worcestershire sauce, salad dressings, ketchup, mayonnaise, and marinades. You can also make your own sauces and dressings using gluten-free ingredients.

5. Canned Goods: Keep your pantry stocked with gluten-free canned goods such as beans, lentils, canned tomatoes, and canned vegetables. These ingredients are versatile, convenient, and can be used in various recipes, including soups, stews, and salads.

6. Nut Butters and Spreads: Peanut butter, almond butter, and other nut butters are typically gluten-free and make great additions to a gluten-free pantry. Look for options without added gluten-containing ingredients. Consider stocking up on gluten-free spreads like fruit preserves, honey, maple syrup, and nutella.

7. Baking Essentials: Ensure you have gluten-free baking essentials like baking powder, baking soda, xanthan gum (a common gluten substitute), yeast, and vanilla extract. These items are crucial for gluten-free baking and help achieve the desired texture and flavor in baked goods.

8. Nuts, Seeds, and Dried Fruits: These make for healthy and gluten-free snacks, as well as ingredients for baking and cooking. Stock up on a variety of nuts (such as almonds, walnuts, and cashews), seeds (like chia, flax, and sunflower seeds), and dried fruits (such as raisins, cranberries, and apricots).

9. Gluten-Free Snacks: Include a selection of gluten-free snacks in your pantry for quick and convenient options. Look for gluten-free granola bars, rice cakes, popcorn, gluten-free crackers, and snack mixes. However, always check the ingredient labels to ensure they are truly gluten-free.

10. Herbs, Spices, and Seasonings: Build a collection of herbs, spices, and seasonings to add flavor to your gluten-free dishes. Having a variety of options like salt, pepper, garlic powder, onion powder, dried herbs (such as basil, oregano, and thyme), and spices (like cumin, paprika, and cinnamon) allows you to add depth and variety to your meals.

Remember to always double-check labels and look for gluten-free certification symbols to ensure the products you purchase are truly gluten-free. Regularly inspect your pantry to remove expired items and replenish as needed. With a well-stocked gluten-free pantry, you'll have the foundation for creating delicious and satisfying gluten-free meals and snacks anytime.

2.2 Essential Cooking Tools

Having the right cooking tools in your kitchen can make a significant difference in your cooking experience, efficiency, and the quality of your meals. When following a gluten-free lifestyle, it's helpful to have a set of essential cooking tools that cater to your specific needs. Here are some key cooking tools that can assist you in preparing gluten-free meals:

1. Mixing Bowls: A set of mixing bowls in various sizes is essential for combining ingredients, whisking eggs, preparing batters,

and mixing dough. Look for durable and lightweight bowls that are easy to clean.

2. Measuring Cups and Spoons: Accurate measurements are crucial in gluten-free baking and cooking. Invest in a set of measuring cups and spoons for precise measuring of ingredients like flours, liquids, and spices.

3. Chef's Knife: A high-quality chef's knife is a versatile tool that aids in slicing, dicing, and chopping ingredients. It's essential for efficient meal preparation and ensures consistent cuts.

4. Cutting Board: Opt for a cutting board specifically designated for gluten-free food preparation to avoid cross-contamination. Choose a durable, non-porous, and easy-to-clean board made from materials like plastic or bamboo.

5. Baking Sheets and Pans: Having a few baking sheets and pans in different sizes is crucial for gluten-free baking. Look for non-stick options or

use parchment paper to prevent sticking and make cleanup easier.

6. Blender or Food Processor: These appliances are useful for making gluten-free sauces, smoothies, dips, and pureeing ingredients. A blender is ideal for liquids and smooth textures, while a food processor is excellent for chopping, grinding, and mixing.

7. Non-Stick Skillet or Saute Pan: A non-stick skillet or saute pan is helpful for cooking gluten-free grains, sauteing vegetables, frying eggs, and making stir-fries. It requires less oil and ensures that food doesn't stick to the pan.

8. Slow Cooker or Instant Pot: These appliances are time-saving and convenient for cooking gluten-free meals with minimal effort. They are great for making soups, stews, chili, and slow-cooked meats.

9. Whisk: A whisk is a versatile tool for blending ingredients, emulsifying dressings, and

incorporating air into batters. It's handy for gluten-free baking and preparing sauces and dressings.

10. Silicone Spatula: A silicone spatula is heat-resistant, flexible, and ideal for scraping bowls, folding ingredients, and mixing batters. It ensures that no batter is wasted and aids in easy cleanup.

11. Oven Mitts: Protect your hands from hot dishes and pans with reliable oven mitts. Look for heat-resistant mitts that provide a secure grip and allow you to handle hot items safely.

12. Colander: A colander is essential for draining gluten-free pasta, rinsing grains, and washing vegetables. Opt for a sturdy colander with small holes to prevent small grains from slipping through.

13. Can Opener: Choose a durable can opener to easily open canned goods like beans, tomatoes,

and sauces. Look for an opener that leaves smooth edges to prevent accidental cuts.

14. Grater: A grater is useful for grating cheese, vegetables, and zesting citrus fruits. It adds texture and flavor to gluten-free dishes like salads, casseroles, and baked goods.

15. Storage Containers: Invest in a variety of airtight storage containers for storing gluten-free flours, grains, leftovers, and prepped ingredients. They help maintain freshness and prevent cross-contamination.

These essential cooking tools will provide a solid foundation for your gluten-free cooking endeavors. Remember to choose high-quality, durable items that suit your needs and cooking style. With the right tools at your disposal, you'll be well-equipped to create delicious gluten-free meals with ease and confidence.

2.3 Reading Food Labels for Gluten-Free Ingredients

When following a gluten-free diet, reading food labels becomes an essential skill to ensure that the products you choose are free from gluten-containing ingredients. Here are some tips to help you navigate food labels and identify gluten-free ingredients:

1. Look for Gluten-Free Certifications: Some food products carry gluten-free certifications or labels from recognized organizations. These certifications indicate that the product has undergone testing and meets specific gluten-free standards. Look for logos such as the "Certified Gluten-Free" label or similar indications.

2. Check the Ingredients List: The ingredients list is where you'll find crucial information about what's in the product. Scan the list for any obvious sources of gluten, such as wheat, barley, rye, and their derivatives. Keep in mind that gluten can appear under different names, including "malt," "malt extract," "malt vinegar,"

"wheat starch," "barley malt," "rye flour," and others.

3. Be Aware of Cross-Contamination: Cross-contamination can occur when gluten-free products come into contact with gluten-containing products during manufacturing or processing. Look for statements on the packaging that indicate whether the product may contain traces of gluten due to cross-contamination. Statements like "May contain wheat" or "Processed in a facility that also processes wheat" alert you to the possibility of cross-contamination.

4. Look for Gluten-Free Labels: Some manufacturers voluntarily label their products as "gluten-free" to cater to those with dietary restrictions. This label indicates that the product meets the standard for gluten content set by the regulatory authority. However, always double-check the ingredient list even if a product bears a gluten-free label.

5. Familiarize Yourself with Gluten-Free Grains and Ingredients: While gluten is commonly found in wheat, barley, and rye, there are many gluten-free grains and ingredients that can be safely consumed. Become familiar with gluten-free alternatives like rice, quinoa, corn, millet, sorghum, oats (labeled as gluten-free), amaranth, and buckwheat. By recognizing these ingredients, you can easily identify gluten-free options.

6. Watch for Hidden Sources of Gluten: Gluten can sometimes hide in unexpected ingredients or additives. Look out for modified food starch, hydrolyzed vegetable protein (HVP), maltodextrin, caramel color, and dextrin, as these can be derived from gluten-containing sources. It's best to verify with the manufacturer or choose products labeled as gluten-free.

7. Consult Reliable Gluten-Free Resources: Keep reference materials, such as gluten-free food lists or smartphone apps, that provide information about safe and unsafe ingredients.

These resources can serve as a quick reference when you're unsure about specific ingredients.

8. Be Cautious with Generic Terms: Generic terms like "natural flavors" or "spices" on food labels may be derived from gluten-containing sources. While these terms can be gluten-free, it's advisable to contact the manufacturer or seek clarification if you're uncertain about their gluten content.

9. Stay Informed and Updated: Food ingredients and manufacturing practices can change over time. Stay informed about the latest developments in gluten-free labeling regulations and periodically check for updated information on safe gluten-free ingredients.

10. Consult a Registered Dietitian: If you have specific dietary concerns or require additional guidance, consult a registered dietitian who specializes in gluten-free diets. They can provide personalized advice and help you navigate food labels effectively.

Remember, reading food labels is an essential skill when following a gluten-free diet. By being diligent and informed, you can make well-informed choices and select products that align with your dietary needs and preferences.

Chapter 3: Breakfast and Brunch Recipes

3.1 Quinoa Breakfast Bowl

Ingredients:
- 1 cup cooked quinoa
- 1/2 cup unsweetened almond milk (or any milk of your choice)
- 1 tablespoon honey or maple syrup
- 1/2 teaspoon vanilla extract
- 1/4 teaspoon cinnamon
- 1/4 cup fresh berries (such as strawberries, blueberries, or raspberries)
- 1 tablespoon chopped nuts (such as almonds, walnuts, or pecans)
- 1 tablespoon unsweetened shredded coconut
- Optional toppings: sliced banana, chia seeds, hemp seeds, or drizzle of nut butter

Instructions:
1. In a small saucepan, combine the cooked quinoa, almond milk, honey or maple syrup, vanilla extract, and cinnamon. Heat over

medium heat, stirring occasionally, until heated through and well combined.

2. Once the mixture is warmed, remove from heat and transfer to a serving bowl.

3. Top the quinoa mixture with fresh berries, chopped nuts, and shredded coconut.

4. Add any additional desired toppings such as sliced banana, chia seeds, hemp seeds, or a drizzle of nut butter.

5. Give it a gentle stir to mix the toppings with the quinoa.

6. Enjoy your delicious and nutritious Quinoa Breakfast Bowl!

Feel free to customize this recipe by adding your favorite fruits, nuts, or seeds. You can also adjust the sweetness to your liking by adding more or less honey/maple syrup. This recipe provides a balanced and filling breakfast packed with protein, fiber, and healthy fats to start your day off right.

3.2 Banana Oat Pancakes

Ingredients:
- 1 cup rolled oats
- 1 ripe banana
- 2 eggs
- 1/4 cup milk (dairy or non-dairy)
- 1 tablespoon honey or maple syrup
- 1/2 teaspoon vanilla extract
- 1/2 teaspoon baking powder
- 1/4 teaspoon cinnamon (optional)
- Pinch of salt
- Cooking oil or butter for greasing the pan

Instructions:
1. In a blender or food processor, pulse the rolled oats until they reach a flour-like consistency.

2. Add the ripe banana, eggs, milk, honey or maple syrup, vanilla extract, baking powder, cinnamon (if desired), and salt to the blender or

food processor. Blend until all the ingredients are well combined and the batter is smooth.

3. Let the batter rest for about 5 minutes to allow the oats to absorb some of the liquid and thicken slightly.

4. Preheat a non-stick skillet or griddle over medium heat. Lightly grease the surface with cooking oil or butter.

5. Pour about 1/4 cup of the pancake batter onto the preheated skillet for each pancake. You can adjust the size based on your preference.

6. Cook the pancakes for 2-3 minutes, or until bubbles start to form on the surface. Flip the pancakes and cook for an additional 1-2 minutes, or until they are golden brown and cooked through.

7. Remove the pancakes from the skillet and keep them warm. Repeat the process with the

remaining batter, adding more oil or butter to the pan as needed.

8. Serve the banana oat pancakes warm with your favorite toppings such as fresh fruit, a drizzle of honey or maple syrup, yogurt, or nut butter.

These banana oat pancakes are not only delicious but also packed with fiber and nutrients. They're a great way to start your day on a healthy and satisfying note. Enjoy!

3.3 Veggie Breakfast Burrito
Ingredients:
- 1 tablespoon olive oil
- 1/2 medium onion, diced
- 1 bell pepper, diced
- 1 small zucchini, diced
- 1 cup sliced mushrooms
- 1/2 teaspoon ground cumin
- 1/2 teaspoon paprika
- Salt and pepper to taste
- 4 large eggs, beaten

- 4 whole wheat or gluten-free tortillas
- 1/2 cup shredded cheddar cheese (optional)
- Salsa or hot sauce (optional)
- Fresh cilantro, chopped (optional)

Instructions:

1. In a large skillet, heat the olive oil over medium heat. Add the diced onion, bell pepper, zucchini, and mushrooms. Sauté for about 5 minutes until the vegetables are tender.

2. Sprinkle the ground cumin, paprika, salt, and pepper over the sautéed vegetables. Stir well to coat the vegetables with the spices.

3. Push the vegetables to one side of the skillet and pour the beaten eggs onto the other side. Cook the eggs, stirring occasionally, until they are scrambled and fully cooked.

4. Once the eggs are cooked, combine them with the sautéed vegetables in the skillet. Stir everything together to ensure the vegetables and eggs are evenly mixed.

5. Warm the tortillas in a separate skillet or in the microwave according to the package instructions.

6. Divide the vegetable and egg mixture evenly among the warmed tortillas. Sprinkle shredded cheese (if using) over the filling.

7. Optional: Add salsa or hot sauce for an extra kick of flavor.

8. Roll up the tortillas tightly, tucking in the sides as you go, to form the breakfast burritos.

9. If desired, lightly toast the burritos in a skillet for a few minutes on each side to make them crispy.

10. Serve the veggie breakfast burritos warm, garnished with fresh chopped cilantro, and enjoy!

These veggie breakfast burritos are not only delicious and satisfying but also packed with nutritious vegetables. Feel free to customize the recipe by adding other veggies of your choice, such as spinach, tomatoes, or corn. They are perfect for a quick and healthy breakfast on the go.

3.4 Gluten-Free Granola Bars

Ingredients:
- 2 cups gluten-free rolled oats
- 1/2 cup unsweetened shredded coconut
- 1/2 cup chopped nuts (such as almonds, walnuts, or cashews)
- 1/2 cup dried fruit (such as raisins, cranberries, or chopped apricots)
- 1/4 cup honey or maple syrup
- 1/4 cup nut butter (such as almond butter or peanut butter)
- 2 tablespoons coconut oil
- 1 teaspoon vanilla extract
- 1/4 teaspoon salt

Instructions:

1. Preheat your oven to 350°F (175°C) and line a baking dish with parchment paper.

2. In a large mixing bowl, combine the gluten-free rolled oats, shredded coconut, chopped nuts, and dried fruit. Mix well.

3. In a small saucepan, heat the honey or maple syrup, nut butter, coconut oil, vanilla extract, and salt over low heat. Stir until the mixture is smooth and well combined.

4. Pour the liquid mixture over the dry ingredients in the mixing bowl. Stir until all the ingredients are evenly coated.

5. Transfer the mixture to the prepared baking dish and press it down firmly using the back of a spoon or spatula. Ensure it is packed tightly and evenly.

6. Bake in the preheated oven for about 15-20 minutes or until the edges turn golden brown.

7. Remove the baking dish from the oven and let it cool completely. This will allow the granola bars to firm up.

8. Once cooled, lift the parchment paper to remove the solidified granola bar mixture from the baking dish. Place it on a cutting board and slice it into bars or squares of your desired size.

9. Store the gluten-free granola bars in an airtight container at room temperature or in the refrigerator for freshness.

These homemade gluten-free granola bars are a great option for a quick and nutritious snack. You can customize the recipe by adding ingredients like chocolate chips, seeds, or spices, based on your preference. Enjoy the wholesome goodness of these delicious bars!

3.5 Overnight Chia Pudding
Ingredients:
- 1/4 cup chia seeds
- 1 cup milk (dairy or non-dairy)

- 1 tablespoon honey or maple syrup (optional, for sweetness)
- 1/2 teaspoon vanilla extract
- Fresh fruits, nuts, or seeds for toppings (optional)

Instructions:
1. In a bowl or jar, combine the chia seeds, milk, honey or maple syrup (if using), and vanilla extract. Stir well to ensure that the chia seeds are evenly distributed.

2. Let the mixture sit for about 5 minutes, then give it another stir to prevent clumping of the chia seeds.

3. Cover the bowl or jar and refrigerate overnight or for at least 4 hours to allow the chia seeds to absorb the liquid and thicken.

4. After the pudding has set, give it a good stir to break up any clumps and achieve a smooth consistency.

5. If desired, you can add additional toppings such as fresh fruits (e.g., berries, sliced banana), nuts (e.g., almonds, walnuts), or seeds (e.g., flaxseeds, pumpkin seeds) for added flavor and texture.

6. Serve the overnight chia pudding chilled and enjoy!

Note: You can adjust the sweetness and thickness of the pudding by adding more or less honey/maple syrup and milk, respectively. Feel free to experiment with different flavors by adding spices like cinnamon or cocoa powder.

Overnight chia pudding is not only a delicious and satisfying breakfast option but also packed with fiber, omega-3 fatty acids, and various nutrients. It's a versatile recipe that allows for endless customization with different toppings and flavors. Enjoy the creamy goodness of this nutritious pudding!

Chapter 4: Lunch and Dinner Recipes

4.1 Mediterranean Quinoa Salad

Ingredients:
- 1 cup cooked quinoa
- 1 cup cherry tomatoes, halved
- 1 cucumber, diced
- 1/2 red onion, thinly sliced
- 1/2 cup pitted Kalamata olives, halved
- 1/2 cup crumbled feta cheese
- 1/4 cup chopped fresh parsley
- 1/4 cup chopped fresh mint
- Juice of 1 lemon
- 2 tablespoons extra-virgin olive oil
- Salt and pepper to taste

Instructions:
1. In a large mixing bowl, combine the cooked quinoa, cherry tomatoes, cucumber, red onion, Kalamata olives, feta cheese, parsley, and mint. Toss gently to mix the ingredients.

2. In a small bowl, whisk together the lemon juice, olive oil, salt, and pepper to make the dressing.

3. Pour the dressing over the quinoa salad and toss well to coat all the ingredients with the dressing.

4. Taste the salad and adjust the seasoning with additional salt and pepper if needed.

5. Allow the Mediterranean Quinoa Salad to sit for at least 10-15 minutes before serving. This allows the flavors to meld together.

6. Serve the salad chilled or at room temperature as a refreshing side dish or a light meal.

You can also customize this recipe by adding other Mediterranean ingredients like diced bell peppers, artichoke hearts, or sun-dried tomatoes. This colorful and nutritious salad is packed with fresh flavors and makes a perfect addition to your summer meals or as a potluck dish. Enjoy the vibrant taste of the Mediterranean!

4.2 Gluten-Free Pizza

Ingredients for the Pizza Crust:
- 2 cups gluten-free all-purpose flour blend
- 1 teaspoon xanthan gum (if not already included in the flour blend)
- 1 teaspoon instant yeast
- 1 teaspoon sugar
- 1 teaspoon salt
- 1 cup warm water
- 2 tablespoons olive oil
- 1 teaspoon apple cider vinegar

Ingredients for the Pizza Toppings:
- 1/2 cup pizza sauce or marinara sauce
- 1 1/2 cups shredded mozzarella cheese (or dairy-free alternative)
- Your choice of toppings such as sliced bell peppers, onions, mushrooms, olives, spinach, cooked chicken, or pepperoni (ensure they are gluten-free if needed)
- Fresh basil leaves for garnish (optional)

Instructions:

1. In a large mixing bowl, combine the gluten-free all-purpose flour, xanthan gum (if needed), instant yeast, sugar, and salt. Mix well.

2. In a separate bowl, combine the warm water, olive oil, and apple cider vinegar.

3. Gradually pour the wet ingredients into the dry ingredients while stirring. Mix until a sticky dough forms.

4. Cover the bowl with a clean kitchen towel and let the dough rest for 30 minutes. This will allow it to rise slightly.

5. Preheat your oven to 425°F (220°C) and line a baking sheet with parchment paper.

6. Transfer the dough onto the prepared baking sheet. Wet your hands with water or lightly oil them to prevent sticking, then press and shape

the dough into a round or rectangular pizza crust of your desired thickness.

7. Bake the crust in the preheated oven for about 10-12 minutes, or until it starts to turn golden brown.

8. Remove the partially baked crust from the oven and spread the pizza sauce evenly over the surface.

9. Sprinkle the shredded mozzarella cheese on top of the sauce, followed by your chosen toppings.

10. Return the pizza to the oven and bake for an additional 10-12 minutes, or until the cheese is melted and bubbly, and the toppings are cooked to your liking.

11. Once the pizza is done, remove it from the oven and let it cool for a few minutes. This allows the crust to firm up slightly before slicing.

12. Garnish with fresh basil leaves, if desired, and serve the delicious gluten-free pizza slices while still warm.

Feel free to get creative with the toppings and experiment with different combinations to suit your taste preferences. Enjoy your homemade gluten-free pizza, and savor every delicious bite!

4.3 Chicken and Vegetable Stir-Fry
Ingredients:
- 2 chicken breasts, thinly sliced
- 2 tablespoons soy sauce (gluten-free if needed)
- 1 tablespoon cornstarch
- 2 tablespoons vegetable oil, divided
- 2 cloves garlic, minced
- 1 teaspoon grated ginger
- 1 bell pepper, thinly sliced
- 1 carrot, thinly sliced
- 1 cup broccoli florets
- 1 cup snap peas
- 1/4 cup chicken broth or water
- Salt and pepper to taste

- Optional garnish: sliced green onions, sesame seeds

Instructions:
1. In a bowl, combine the sliced chicken breasts, soy sauce, and cornstarch. Mix well to coat the chicken evenly. Let it marinate for about 10-15 minutes.

2. Heat 1 tablespoon of vegetable oil in a large skillet or wok over medium-high heat.

3. Add the marinated chicken to the skillet and stir-fry for 5-6 minutes, or until the chicken is cooked through and slightly browned. Remove the cooked chicken from the skillet and set it aside.

4. In the same skillet, add the remaining 1 tablespoon of vegetable oil. Add the minced garlic and grated ginger, and stir-fry for about 1 minute until fragrant.

5. Add the sliced bell pepper, carrot, broccoli florets, and snap peas to the skillet. Stir-fry for 3-4 minutes, or until the vegetables are tender-crisp.

6. Pour in the chicken broth or water to deglaze the skillet, scraping up any browned bits from the bottom. This will add flavor to the stir-fry.

7. Return the cooked chicken to the skillet with the vegetables. Stir everything together.

8. Season with salt and pepper to taste. Adjust the seasoning or add more soy sauce if desired.

9. Continue to stir-fry for another 1-2 minutes, allowing the flavors to meld together.

10. Remove the skillet from the heat. Garnish with sliced green onions and sesame seeds if desired.

11. Serve the chicken and vegetable stir-fry hot over steamed rice or noodles.

This chicken and vegetable stir-fry is a quick and healthy meal option that's packed with flavor and nutrients. You can customize the vegetables based on your preference or what you have on hand. Enjoy the delicious combination of tender chicken and vibrant vegetables in this satisfying dish!

4.4 Zucchini Noodles with Pesto
Ingredients:
- 3-4 medium zucchini
- 1/2 cup fresh basil leaves
- 1/4 cup pine nuts
- 2 cloves garlic
- 1/4 cup grated Parmesan cheese (optional)
- 1/4 cup extra-virgin olive oil
- Juice of 1/2 lemon
- Salt and pepper to taste
- Optional toppings: cherry tomatoes, sliced almonds, additional Parmesan cheese

Instructions:

1. Start by spiralizing the zucchini into noodles using a spiralizer. If you don't have a spiralizer, you can use a julienne peeler or simply slice the zucchini into thin strips resembling noodles. Set aside.

2. In a food processor or blender, combine the fresh basil leaves, pine nuts, garlic, and Parmesan cheese (if using). Pulse until the ingredients are well chopped and blended.

3. While the food processor is running, slowly drizzle in the olive oil until a smooth and creamy pesto sauce is formed. Add the lemon juice, salt, and pepper, and pulse briefly to combine.

4. In a large skillet, heat a small amount of olive oil over medium heat. Add the zucchini noodles and sauté for about 2-3 minutes, or until they are just tender. Be careful not to overcook them, as they can become mushy.

5. Remove the skillet from the heat and add the prepared pesto sauce to the zucchini noodles.

Toss well to coat the noodles evenly with the pesto.

6. Taste and adjust the seasoning if needed, adding more salt, pepper, or lemon juice according to your preference.

7. Optional: You can add cherry tomatoes, sliced almonds, or additional grated Parmesan cheese as toppings for extra flavor and texture.

8. Serve the zucchini noodles with pesto immediately while they are still warm.

This zucchini noodles with pesto recipe is a light and refreshing alternative to traditional pasta dishes. It's low in carbs and packed with fresh flavors. Enjoy this healthy and delicious meal option!

4.5 Black Bean Tacos with Avocado Salsa
Ingredients for Black Bean Filling:
- 1 tablespoon olive oil
- 1 small onion, diced

- 2 cloves garlic, minced
- 1 teaspoon ground cumin
- 1 teaspoon chili powder
- 1 can (15 ounces) black beans, rinsed and drained
- Salt and pepper to taste

Ingredients for Avocado Salsa:
- 1 ripe avocado, peeled, pitted, and diced
- 1 small tomato, diced
- 1/4 cup red onion, finely chopped
- 1/4 cup fresh cilantro, chopped
- Juice of 1 lime
- Salt and pepper to taste

Additional Taco Ingredients:
- Corn or flour tortillas (gluten-free if needed)
- Shredded lettuce or cabbage
- Diced tomatoes
- Optional toppings: sour cream, shredded cheese, hot sauce

Instructions:

1. In a skillet, heat olive oil over medium heat. Add diced onion and minced garlic, and sauté until the onion becomes translucent.

2. Add ground cumin and chili powder to the skillet, and stir for about 1 minute to toast the spices and release their flavors.

3. Add the rinsed and drained black beans to the skillet. Season with salt and pepper. Cook the beans for about 5 minutes, stirring occasionally, until they are heated through and well-coated with the spices.

4. While the black bean filling is cooking, prepare the avocado salsa. In a bowl, combine diced avocado, tomato, red onion, cilantro, lime juice, salt, and pepper. Gently toss to combine all the ingredients.

5. Warm the corn or flour tortillas in a dry skillet or microwave.

6. Assemble the tacos by spooning the black bean filling onto each tortilla. Top with shredded lettuce or cabbage, diced tomatoes, and a generous spoonful of avocado salsa.

7. Optional: Add your desired toppings such as sour cream, shredded cheese, or hot sauce.

8. Serve the black bean tacos with avocado salsa immediately and enjoy!

These black bean tacos with avocado salsa are not only delicious but also packed with protein, fiber, and fresh flavors. They make a satisfying and healthy meal option for any day of the week. Customize the toppings and add your favorite ingredients to make it your own. Bon appétit!

4.6 Thai Curry Rice Noodles
Ingredients:
- 8 ounces rice noodles
- 1 tablespoon vegetable oil
- 1 small onion, thinly sliced
- 2 cloves garlic, minced

- 1 red bell pepper, thinly sliced
- 1 carrot, julienned
- 1 cup broccoli florets
- 1 cup snap peas
- 1 can (13.5 ounces) coconut milk
- 2 tablespoons Thai red curry paste
- 1 tablespoon soy sauce (gluten-free if needed)
- 1 tablespoon brown sugar
- Juice of 1 lime
- Fresh cilantro and lime wedges for garnish (optional)

Instructions:
1. Cook the rice noodles according to the package instructions. Drain and set aside.

2. In a large skillet or wok, heat the vegetable oil over medium heat.

3. Add the sliced onion and minced garlic to the skillet. Sauté for 2-3 minutes until the onion becomes translucent and the garlic is fragrant.

4. Add the red bell pepper, julienned carrot, broccoli florets, and snap peas to the skillet. Stir-fry for 3-4 minutes until the vegetables are crisp-tender.

5. In a small bowl, whisk together the coconut milk, Thai red curry paste, soy sauce, brown sugar, and lime juice.

6. Pour the curry mixture into the skillet with the vegetables. Stir well to combine and let it simmer for 2-3 minutes to allow the flavors to meld together.

7. Add the cooked rice noodles to the skillet. Toss gently to coat the noodles evenly with the curry sauce and heat through.

8. Taste and adjust the seasoning with more soy sauce, brown sugar, or lime juice if desired.

9. Optional: Garnish with fresh cilantro and serve with lime wedges for an extra burst of flavor.

10. Serve the Thai curry rice noodles hot as a main dish or side dish.

These Thai curry rice noodles are bursting with aromatic flavors and offer a delightful blend of textures from the vegetables and rice noodles. Feel free to customize the spice level by adjusting the amount of curry paste to your taste. Enjoy this delicious and satisfying Thai-inspired dish!

Chapter 5: Snacks and Sides

5.1 Baked Sweet Potato Fries

Ingredients:
- 2 large sweet potatoes
- 2 tablespoons olive oil
- 1 teaspoon paprika
- 1/2 teaspoon garlic powder
- 1/2 teaspoon salt
- 1/4 teaspoon black pepper
- Optional toppings: grated Parmesan cheese, chopped fresh parsley

Instructions:

1. Preheat your oven to 425°F (220°C) and line a baking sheet with parchment paper.

2. Wash the sweet potatoes and pat them dry with a clean towel. Leave the skin on for added texture and nutrients.

3. Cut the sweet potatoes into evenly sized strips, resembling French fries. Try to make

them similar in thickness to ensure even cooking.

4. Place the sweet potato fries in a large bowl. Drizzle with olive oil and toss to coat them evenly.

5. In a small bowl, mix together the paprika, garlic powder, salt, and black pepper. Sprinkle the spice mixture over the sweet potato fries and toss again to ensure they are well coated.

6. Arrange the seasoned sweet potato fries in a single layer on the prepared baking sheet, ensuring they have space between them for even browning.

7. Bake in the preheated oven for 20-25 minutes, flipping the fries halfway through. They should be golden brown and crispy on the outside.

8. Remove the baking sheet from the oven and let the sweet potato fries cool slightly.

9. Optional: Sprinkle grated Parmesan cheese and chopped fresh parsley over the fries for added flavor and visual appeal.

10. Serve the baked sweet potato fries as a side dish or a healthy snack.

These baked sweet potato fries are a nutritious alternative to traditional fries and are packed with natural sweetness. They make a great accompaniment to burgers, sandwiches, or enjoyed on their own. Enjoy the crispy exterior and tender interior of these delightful fries!

5.2 Guacamole and Corn Chips
Ingredients for Guacamole:
- 2 ripe avocados
- 1 small tomato, diced
- 1/4 cup red onion, finely chopped
- 1/4 cup fresh cilantro, chopped
- Juice of 1 lime
- 1 clove garlic, minced
- 1/2 teaspoon salt
- 1/4 teaspoon black pepper

- Optional: 1 jalapeño pepper, seeded and finely chopped (for added heat)

Ingredients for Corn Chips:
- Corn tortillas (gluten-free if needed)
- Vegetable oil for frying
- Salt to taste

Instructions for Guacamole:
1. Cut the avocados in half lengthwise, remove the pits, and scoop the flesh into a bowl.

2. Mash the avocados with a fork until desired consistency is reached. Some prefer chunky guacamole, while others prefer it smooth.

3. Add the diced tomato, red onion, cilantro, lime juice, minced garlic, salt, black pepper, and optional jalapeño pepper to the bowl. Stir gently to combine all the ingredients.

4. Taste the guacamole and adjust the seasoning with more salt, lime juice, or spices if desired.

5. Cover the bowl with plastic wrap, making sure the wrap touches the surface of the guacamole to prevent browning. Refrigerate for at least 30 minutes to allow the flavors to meld together.

Instructions for Corn Chips:
1. Preheat vegetable oil in a deep pot or skillet to 350°F (175°C).

2. While the oil is heating, stack several corn tortillas together and cut them into triangular shapes, resembling chips.

3. Fry the corn chips in batches for about 2-3 minutes, or until they turn golden brown and crispy. Stir occasionally to ensure even frying.

4. Using a slotted spoon or tongs, transfer the fried chips to a paper towel-lined plate to drain excess oil.

5. Immediately sprinkle the hot corn chips with salt to enhance the flavor.

6. Repeat the frying process with the remaining corn chips until all are cooked.

7. Serve the freshly made corn chips alongside the chilled guacamole.

Enjoy the creamy and flavorful guacamole with the crispy corn chips as a tasty appetizer, party snack, or a delicious addition to any Mexican-inspired meal. Dip the chips into the guacamole and savor the combination of creamy avocado, tangy lime, and vibrant herbs and spices.

5.3 Caprese Skewers

Ingredients:
- Cherry or grape tomatoes
- Fresh mozzarella cheese, cut into bite-sized pieces
- Fresh basil leaves
- Balsamic glaze or balsamic reduction
- Salt and pepper to taste
- Skewers or toothpicks

Instructions:

1. Start by rinsing the cherry or grape tomatoes and patting them dry. Set them aside.

2. Cut the fresh mozzarella cheese into bite-sized pieces that are similar in size to the tomatoes.

3. Take a skewer or toothpick and thread one cherry tomato onto it, followed by a piece of mozzarella cheese and a fresh basil leaf. Repeat this pattern until the skewer is filled, leaving a small space at the end for easy handling.

4. Repeat the process with the remaining ingredients to make more Caprese skewers.

5. Place the assembled skewers on a serving platter or plate.

6. Drizzle the Caprese skewers with balsamic glaze or balsamic reduction. You can create a zigzag pattern or simply drizzle a small amount over each skewer.

7. Season the skewers with salt and pepper to taste.

8. Optional: Garnish with additional fresh basil leaves for an extra pop of green and freshness.

9. Serve the Caprese skewers as an appetizer or finger food for your guests to enjoy.

These Caprese skewers are a delightful combination of sweet cherry tomatoes, creamy mozzarella cheese, and fragrant basil. The balsamic glaze adds a tangy and slightly sweet note to enhance the flavors. They are perfect for gatherings, parties, or as a light and refreshing snack. Enjoy these bite-sized treats!

5.4 Oven-Roasted Chickpeas:
Ingredients:
- 1 can (15 ounces) chickpeas (garbanzo beans), drained and rinsed
- 1 tablespoon olive oil
- 1/2 teaspoon ground cumin

- 1/2 teaspoon paprika
- 1/2 teaspoon garlic powder
- 1/4 teaspoon salt
- 1/4 teaspoon black pepper
- Optional seasonings: chili powder, cayenne pepper, dried herbs (such as rosemary or thyme)

Instructions:
1. Preheat your oven to 400°F (200°C) and line a baking sheet with parchment paper.

2. Drain and rinse the chickpeas thoroughly. Pat them dry with a clean towel to remove any excess moisture.

3. In a bowl, combine the chickpeas, olive oil, cumin, paprika, garlic powder, salt, and black pepper. Toss well to ensure all the chickpeas are coated with the seasonings.

4. Optional: If you'd like to add extra flavor, you can sprinkle chili powder, cayenne pepper, or dried herbs over the chickpeas and mix them in.

5. Spread the seasoned chickpeas in a single layer on the prepared baking sheet.

6. Roast the chickpeas in the preheated oven for about 25-30 minutes, stirring them halfway through the cooking time. They should become golden brown and crispy.

7. Once roasted, remove the baking sheet from the oven and let the chickpeas cool slightly.

8. Taste and adjust the seasoning if needed, adding more salt or spices according to your preference.

9. Serve the oven-roasted chickpeas as a crunchy and flavorful snack. They can also be sprinkled over salads or used as a topping for soups.

Oven-roasted chickpeas are a healthy and satisfying alternative to traditional snacks. Enjoy their crispy texture and savory taste, and feel free to experiment with different seasonings to create your own unique flavor combinations. Happy snacking!

5.5 Greek Yogurt Parfait

Ingredients:
- 1 cup Greek yogurt
- 1 tablespoon honey or maple syrup
- 1/2 teaspoon vanilla extract
- 1/2 cup granola
- 1/2 cup mixed fresh berries (such as strawberries, blueberries, raspberries)
- Optional toppings: chopped nuts, shredded coconut, drizzle of chocolate sauce

Instructions:

1. In a bowl, mix the Greek yogurt, honey or maple syrup, and vanilla extract until well combined. This will be the base of your parfait.

2. Take a glass or a jar and begin layering the ingredients. Start with a spoonful of the Greek yogurt mixture at the bottom.

3. Add a layer of granola on top of the yogurt. You can use your favorite store-bought granola or make your own.

4. Follow with a layer of mixed fresh berries. Use a variety of berries for a burst of color and flavor.

5. Repeat the layers until you reach the top of the glass or jar, ending with a dollop of the Greek yogurt mixture.

6. Optional: Sprinkle chopped nuts, shredded coconut, or drizzle a bit of chocolate sauce on top for added texture and indulgence.

7. Serve the Greek Yogurt Parfait immediately, or refrigerate it for a couple of hours to allow the flavors to meld together.

Enjoy this Greek Yogurt Parfait as a wholesome breakfast, snack, or even as a light dessert. The creamy Greek yogurt, sweet honey or maple syrup, crunchy granola, and fresh berries create a delightful combination of textures and flavors. Customize your parfait with your favorite toppings and enjoy!

Chapter 6: Desserts and Treats

6.1 Flourless Chocolate Brownies

Ingredients:
- 1 cup semisweet chocolate chips
- 1/2 cup unsalted butter
- 3/4 cup granulated sugar
- 1/4 cup unsweetened cocoa powder
- 3 large eggs
- 1 teaspoon vanilla extract
- 1/4 teaspoon salt
- Optional toppings: powdered sugar, chocolate ganache, whipped cream, fresh berries

Instructions:

1. Preheat your oven to 350°F (175°C). Grease a square baking dish or line it with parchment paper.

2. In a microwave-safe bowl, melt the chocolate chips and butter together in the microwave, stirring every 20-30 seconds until smooth and

well combined. Alternatively, you can melt them in a double boiler on the stove.

3. In a separate mixing bowl, whisk together the granulated sugar, cocoa powder, eggs, vanilla extract, and salt until well combined.

4. Pour the melted chocolate mixture into the bowl with the sugar and egg mixture. Stir until the batter is smooth and all the ingredients are fully incorporated.

5. Transfer the batter to the prepared baking dish, spreading it out evenly.

6. Bake in the preheated oven for approximately 25-30 minutes, or until a toothpick inserted into the center comes out with a few moist crumbs. Be careful not to overbake, as you want the brownies to remain fudgy and moist.

7. Remove the baking dish from the oven and let the brownies cool completely in the dish.

8. Once cooled, cut the brownies into squares or rectangles.

9. Optional: Dust the brownies with powdered sugar, drizzle with chocolate ganache, top with whipped cream, or serve with fresh berries for added indulgence.

These flourless chocolate brownies are rich, fudgy, and full of intense chocolate flavor. They are perfect for chocolate lovers and those following a gluten-free diet. Enjoy these delightful treats as a decadent dessert or a sweet pick-me-up throughout the day!

6.2 Peanut Butter Energy Balls
Ingredients:
- 1 cup rolled oats
- 1/2 cup peanut butter (or any nut butter of your choice)
- 1/4 cup honey or maple syrup
- 1/4 cup mini chocolate chips or chopped nuts (optional)
- 1/4 cup flaxseeds or chia seeds

- 1 teaspoon vanilla extract

Instructions:
1. In a large mixing bowl, combine the rolled oats, peanut butter, honey or maple syrup, mini chocolate chips or chopped nuts (if using), flaxseeds or chia seeds, and vanilla extract.

2. Stir the ingredients together until they are well combined. If the mixture seems too dry, you can add a little more peanut butter or honey/maple syrup to help bind the ingredients.

3. Once the mixture is well mixed, cover the bowl and place it in the refrigerator for about 30 minutes. Chilling the mixture will make it easier to roll into balls.

4. After the mixture has chilled, take it out of the refrigerator. Using your hands, scoop out a tablespoon-sized portion of the mixture and roll it into a ball between your palms. Repeat with the remaining mixture.

5. Place the rolled energy balls on a baking sheet or plate lined with parchment paper.

6. Once all the mixture has been rolled into balls, you can enjoy them right away or store them in an airtight container in the refrigerator for later.

These Peanut Butter Energy Balls are a delicious and nutritious snack that provides a boost of energy. Packed with oats, peanut butter, and seeds, they are a great source of fiber, protein, and healthy fats. Enjoy them as a quick pick-me-up during the day or as a pre-workout snack.

6.3 Raspberry Chia Seed Pudding
Ingredients:
- 1/2 cup chia seeds
- 2 cups unsweetened almond milk (or any milk of your choice)
- 1 tablespoon honey or maple syrup
- 1 teaspoon vanilla extract
- 1 cup fresh raspberries (or frozen raspberries, thawed)

- Optional toppings: additional fresh raspberries, shredded coconut, chopped nuts

Instructions:
1. In a mixing bowl, combine the chia seeds, almond milk, honey or maple syrup, and vanilla extract. Stir well to ensure the chia seeds are evenly distributed.

2. Let the mixture sit for about 5 minutes, then give it another stir. This will prevent clumping of the chia seeds.

3. Cover the bowl and refrigerate the mixture for at least 4 hours or overnight. During this time, the chia seeds will absorb the liquid and create a pudding-like consistency.

4. After the pudding has set, remove it from the refrigerator. Give it a good stir to break up any clumps and evenly distribute the seeds.

5. In a blender or food processor, puree the fresh raspberries until smooth. If using frozen raspberries, thaw them first and then puree.

6. To assemble, you can create layers by alternating between the chia seed pudding and the raspberry puree in serving glasses or jars. Start with a layer of chia seed pudding, followed by a layer of raspberry puree, and continue until the glass or jar is filled.

7. Optional: Top the pudding with additional fresh raspberries, shredded coconut, or chopped nuts for added texture and flavor.

8. Serve the Raspberry Chia Seed Pudding immediately, or refrigerate for another hour to chill and allow the flavors to meld together.

This Raspberry Chia Seed Pudding is a delightful and nutritious dessert or breakfast option. The chia seeds provide fiber and omega-3 fatty acids, while the raspberries add a burst of tangy sweetness. Enjoy the creamy and fruity goodness of this pudding as a healthy and satisfying treat.

6.4 Gluten-Free Apple Crisp

Ingredients:

For the Apple Filling:
- 4-5 medium-sized apples (such as Granny Smith or Honeycrisp), peeled, cored, and sliced
- 2 tablespoons granulated sugar
- 1 tablespoon lemon juice
- 1 teaspoon ground cinnamon
- 1/4 teaspoon ground nutmeg

For the Crumb Topping:
- 1 cup gluten-free rolled oats
- 1/2 cup almond flour
- 1/4 cup packed brown sugar
- 1/4 cup melted unsalted butter or coconut oil
- 1 teaspoon ground cinnamon
- 1/4 teaspoon salt

Instructions:

1. Preheat your oven to 350°F (175°C). Grease a baking dish or pie dish with butter or cooking spray.

2. In a large bowl, combine the sliced apples, granulated sugar, lemon juice, ground cinnamon, and ground nutmeg. Toss well to coat the apple slices evenly.

3. Transfer the apple mixture to the greased baking dish, spreading it out evenly.

4. In another bowl, mix together the gluten-free rolled oats, almond flour, brown sugar, melted butter or coconut oil, ground cinnamon, and salt. Stir until the mixture resembles a crumbly texture.

5. Sprinkle the crumb topping evenly over the apple mixture in the baking dish.

6. Bake in the preheated oven for about 35-40 minutes, or until the apples are tender and the topping is golden brown and crispy.

7. Remove the apple crisp from the oven and let it cool for a few minutes before serving.

8. Serve the Gluten-Free Apple Crisp warm, either on its own or with a scoop of vanilla ice cream or a dollop of whipped cream.

Enjoy the comforting flavors of this Gluten-Free Apple Crisp, with its tender and spiced apple filling and crunchy crumb topping. It's a perfect dessert for the fall season or any time you're craving a delicious and gluten-free treat.

6.5 Mango Coconut Ice Cream

Ingredients:
- 2 ripe mangoes, peeled and pitted
- 1 can (13.5 oz) full-fat coconut milk
- 1/4 cup honey or maple syrup (adjust to taste)
- 1 teaspoon vanilla extract
- Pinch of salt
- Optional toppings: shredded coconut, fresh mango slices, mint leaves

Instructions:

1. Cut the ripe mangoes into chunks and place them in a blender or food processor.

2. Add the coconut milk, honey or maple syrup, vanilla extract, and a pinch of salt to the blender with the mangoes.

3. Blend the mixture until smooth and creamy, ensuring there are no lumps or chunks remaining.

4. Taste the mixture and adjust the sweetness by adding more honey or maple syrup if desired.

5. Pour the mango coconut mixture into an ice cream maker and churn according to the manufacturer's instructions until it reaches a soft-serve consistency. This usually takes about 20-30 minutes.

6. Transfer the churned ice cream into a lidded container and freeze for an additional 2-3 hours to firm up.

7. When ready to serve, let the ice cream sit at room temperature for a few minutes to soften slightly for easier scooping.

8. Scoop the Mango Coconut Ice Cream into bowls or cones. Garnish with shredded coconut, fresh mango slices, or mint leaves, if desired.

Enjoy the tropical flavors of this creamy and refreshing Mango Coconut Ice Cream. The combination of sweet mangoes and rich coconut milk creates a delightful treat that will transport you to a sunny paradise. Indulge in this dairy-free and gluten-free dessert and savor the taste of summer!

Chapter 7: Meal Planning And Tips

7.1 Meal Plan

Monday:
- Breakfast: Quinoa Breakfast Bowl
- Lunch: Mediterranean Quinoa Salad
- Dinner: Chicken and Vegetable Stir-Fry
- Snack: Peanut Butter Energy Balls

Tuesday:
- Breakfast: Banana Oat Pancakes
- Lunch: Veggie Breakfast Burrito
- Dinner: Gluten-Free Pizza
- Snack: Greek Yogurt Parfait

Wednesday:
- Breakfast: Overnight Chia Pudding
- Lunch: Black Bean Tacos with Avocado Salsa
- Dinner: Thai Curry Rice Noodles
- Snack: Baked Sweet Potato Fries

Thursday:
- Breakfast: Raspberry Chia Seed Pudding

- Lunch: Zucchini Noodles with Pesto
- Dinner: Chicken and Vegetable Stir-Fry (leftovers)
- Snack: Gluten-Free Granola Bars

Friday:
- Breakfast: Quinoa Breakfast Bowl (leftovers)
- Lunch: Greek Yogurt Parfait
- Dinner: Veggie Breakfast Burrito (leftovers)
- Snack: Oven-Roasted Chickpeas

Saturday:
- Breakfast: Banana Oat Pancakes (leftovers)
- Lunch: Gluten-Free Pizza (leftovers)
- Dinner: Mediterranean Quinoa Salad (leftovers)
- Snack: Guacamole and Corn Chips

Sunday:
- Breakfast: Peanut Butter Energy Balls
- Lunch: Black Bean Tacos with Avocado Salsa (leftovers)
- Dinner: Thai Curry Rice Noodles (leftovers)
- Snack: Greek Yogurt Parfait

Feel free to adjust this meal plan based on your personal preferences and dietary needs. Remember to incorporate fruits, vegetables, and protein sources into your meals to ensure a well-rounded and balanced diet. Enjoy your gluten-free week of delicious and nutritious meals!

7.2 Tips for Meal Prepping on a Budget

Meal prepping on a budget can help you save both time and money while still enjoying delicious and nutritious meals. Here are some tips to help you meal prep on a budget:

1. Plan your meals: Take some time to plan your meals for the week. Look for budget-friendly recipes that use affordable ingredients. Choose recipes that have overlapping ingredients to minimize waste.

2. Make a shopping list: Create a shopping list based on your meal plan and stick to it when you go grocery shopping. Having a list will help you

avoid impulse purchases and stay within your budget.

3. Buy in bulk: Purchase pantry staples like rice, beans, lentils, and oats in bulk. Buying larger quantities is often more cost-effective in the long run. You can portion them out and store them in airtight containers for later use.

4. Utilize seasonal produce: Seasonal fruits and vegetables are often more affordable and have better flavor. Plan your meals around the produce that is in season to save money.

5. Prep ingredients in advance: Wash, chop, and portion out your ingredients ahead of time. This will make cooking during the week more efficient and help reduce food waste.

6. Cook in batches: Prepare large batches of meals that can be divided into individual portions and stored in the fridge or freezer. This way, you can have ready-made meals for busy

days, and it's often more cost-effective than cooking individual meals every day.

7. Repurpose leftovers: Get creative with your leftovers. Turn roasted chicken into sandwiches or salads, and use leftover vegetables in stir-fries or omelets. This helps minimize food waste and saves you from having to cook entirely new meals.

8. Use affordable protein sources: Incorporate affordable protein sources such as beans, lentils, eggs, and canned tuna into your meals. These options are often budget-friendly and provide essential nutrients.

9. Avoid pre-packaged convenience foods: Pre-packaged and processed foods can be costly. Opt for whole, unprocessed ingredients and cook from scratch as much as possible. This allows you to have better control over the ingredients and saves you money.

10. Store and reheat properly: Properly store your prepped meals in airtight containers to maintain freshness and prevent spoilage. Make sure to reheat leftovers thoroughly to ensure food safety.

By following these tips, you can successfully meal prep on a budget and enjoy healthy, homemade meals without breaking the bank.

Conclusion

As you embark on your gluten-free journey, armed with The Gluten-Free Cookbook for College Students: Easy and Delicious Recipes on a Budget, you are equipped with the knowledge and inspiration to create tasty meals that cater to your dietary needs and fit within your college student budget.

The gluten-free lifestyle offers numerous benefits, from improved digestion and increased energy levels to exploring a variety of nutrient-rich ingredients. By embracing gluten-free cooking, you are not only taking care of your health but also discovering a world of delicious and satisfying flavors.

With tips for eating gluten-free on a budget, stocking your pantry, deciphering food labels, and essential cooking tools, you are well-prepared to navigate the gluten-free landscape with confidence and ease. You have learned how to plan your meals, shop smartly, and make the most of your ingredients, all while sticking to your budget.

From mouthwatering breakfasts and satisfying lunches to flavorful dinners and delightful snacks, the cookbook has provided you with a diverse array of recipes to suit every taste and occasion. Whether you're enjoying a comforting bowl of Quinoa Breakfast, savoring the freshness of a Mediterranean Quinoa Salad, or indulging in the decadence of Flourless Chocolate Brownies, each dish is a testament to the delicious possibilities of gluten-free cooking.

As you experiment in the kitchen, remember that the gluten-free lifestyle is not about limitations but rather a chance to explore new ingredients, flavors, and culinary techniques. It is an opportunity to nourish your body with wholesome and nutritious foods while expanding your culinary horizons.

So, embrace this gluten-free journey with enthusiasm and creativity. Let The Gluten-Free

Cookbook for College Students: Easy and Delicious Recipes on a Budget be your companion in the kitchen, empowering you to cook with confidence, eat well, and thrive as you navigate college life. May your meals be filled with joy, delicious flavors, and the knowledge that you are taking care of yourself in the most wholesome and satisfying way.

Happy cooking and bon appétit!

Printed in Great Britain
by Amazon